Copyright © 2015
J. Benson et al

All rights reserved.

ISBN-10: 1519699573
ISBN-13: 978-1519699572

Adult Coloring for Relaxation

Mindful Owls is an adult coloring book containing fifty pages of beautiful patterns designed specifically to help achieve a state of relaxation. Color them in with a pen or pencil to help find your own state of inner peace and tranquility.

Mindful Owls
Adult Coloring for Relaxation

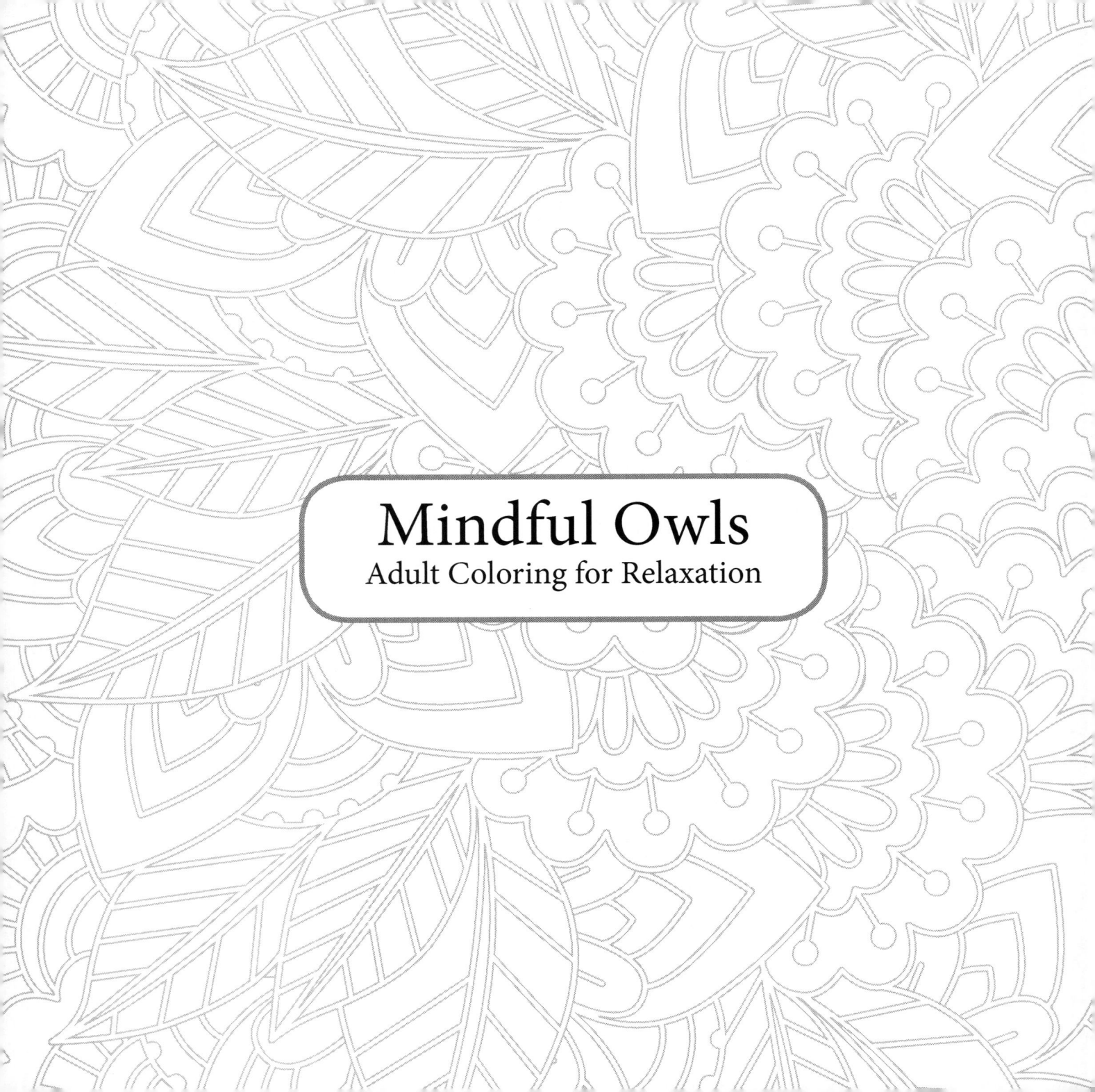

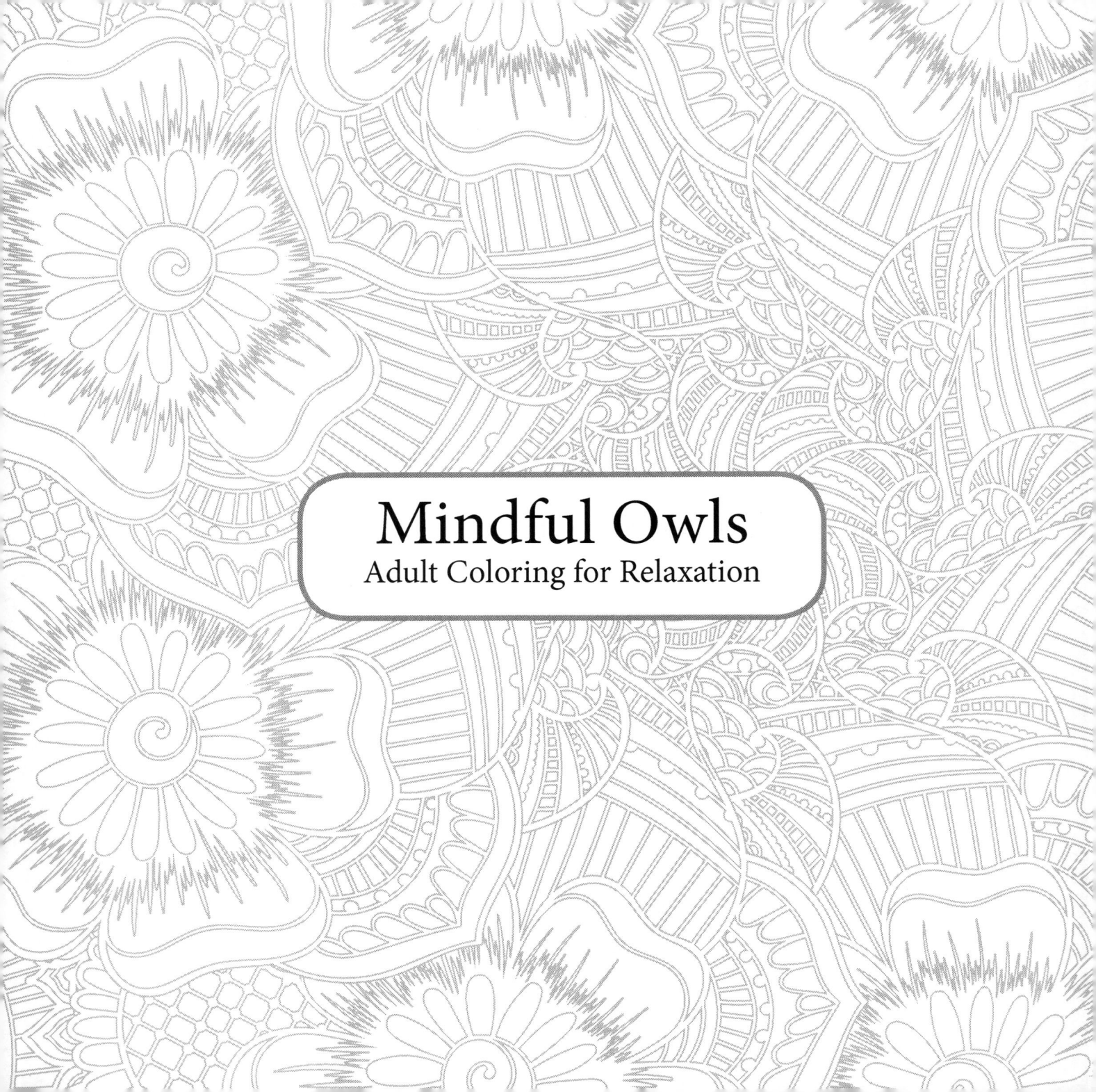

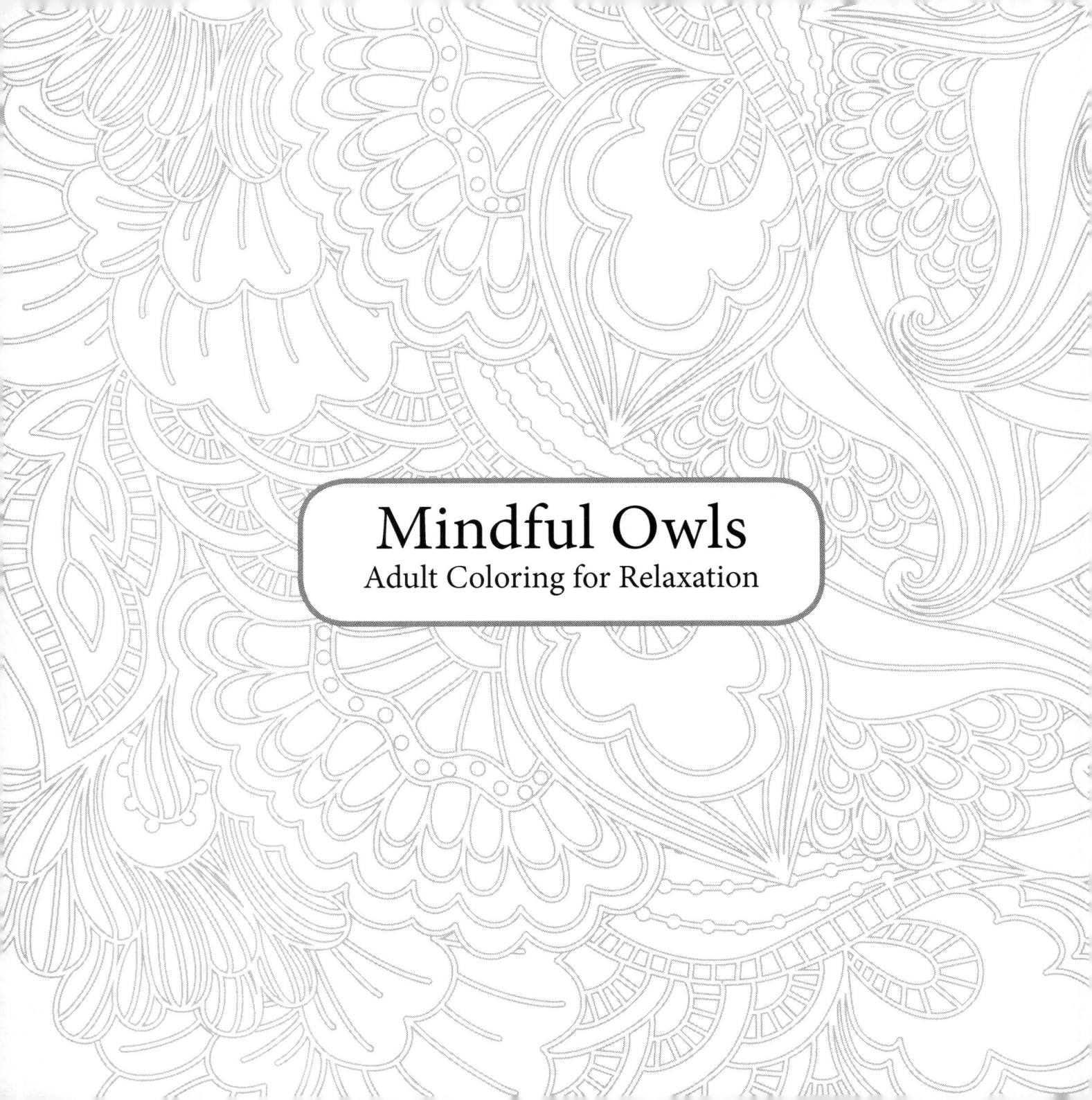

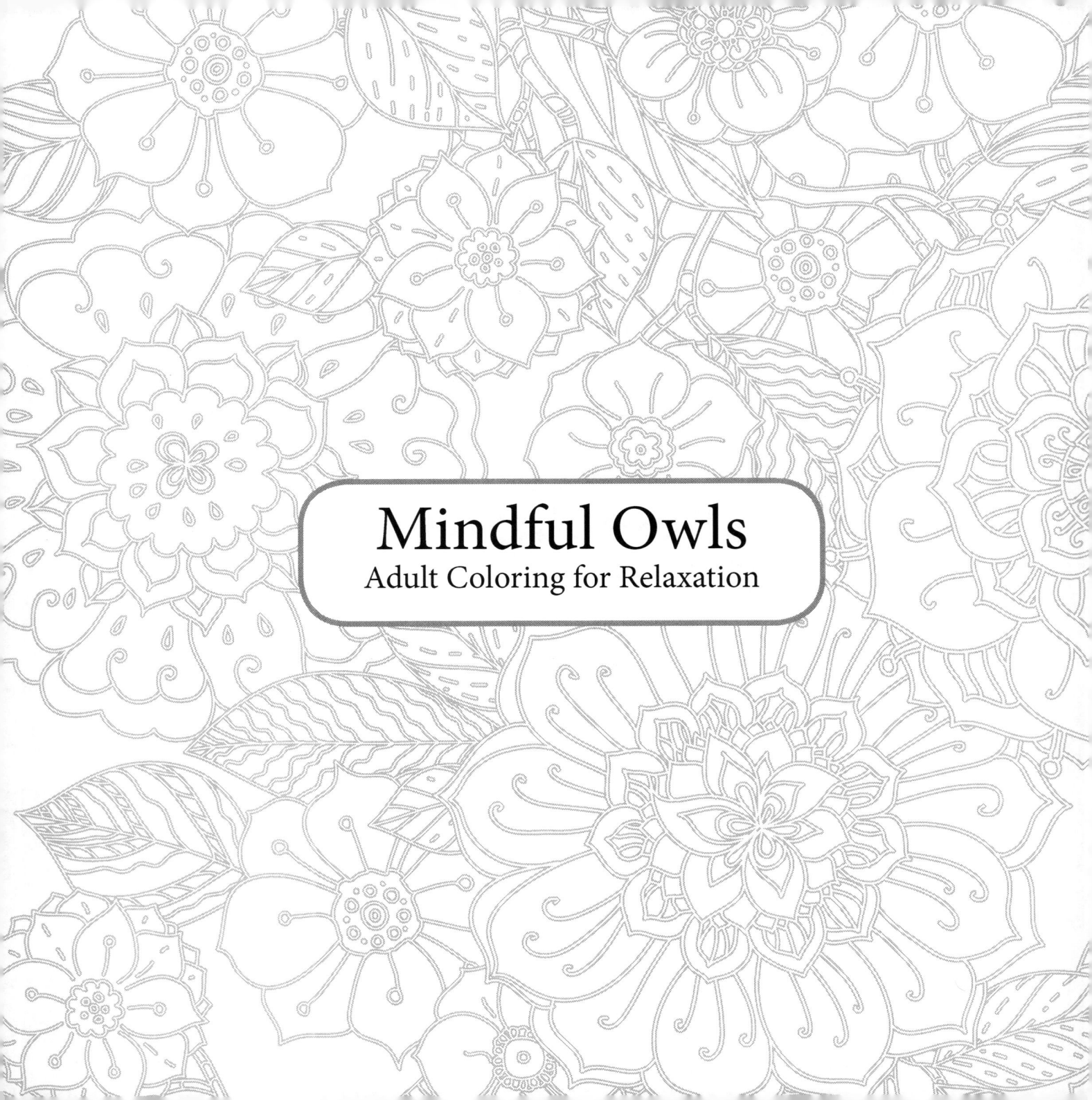

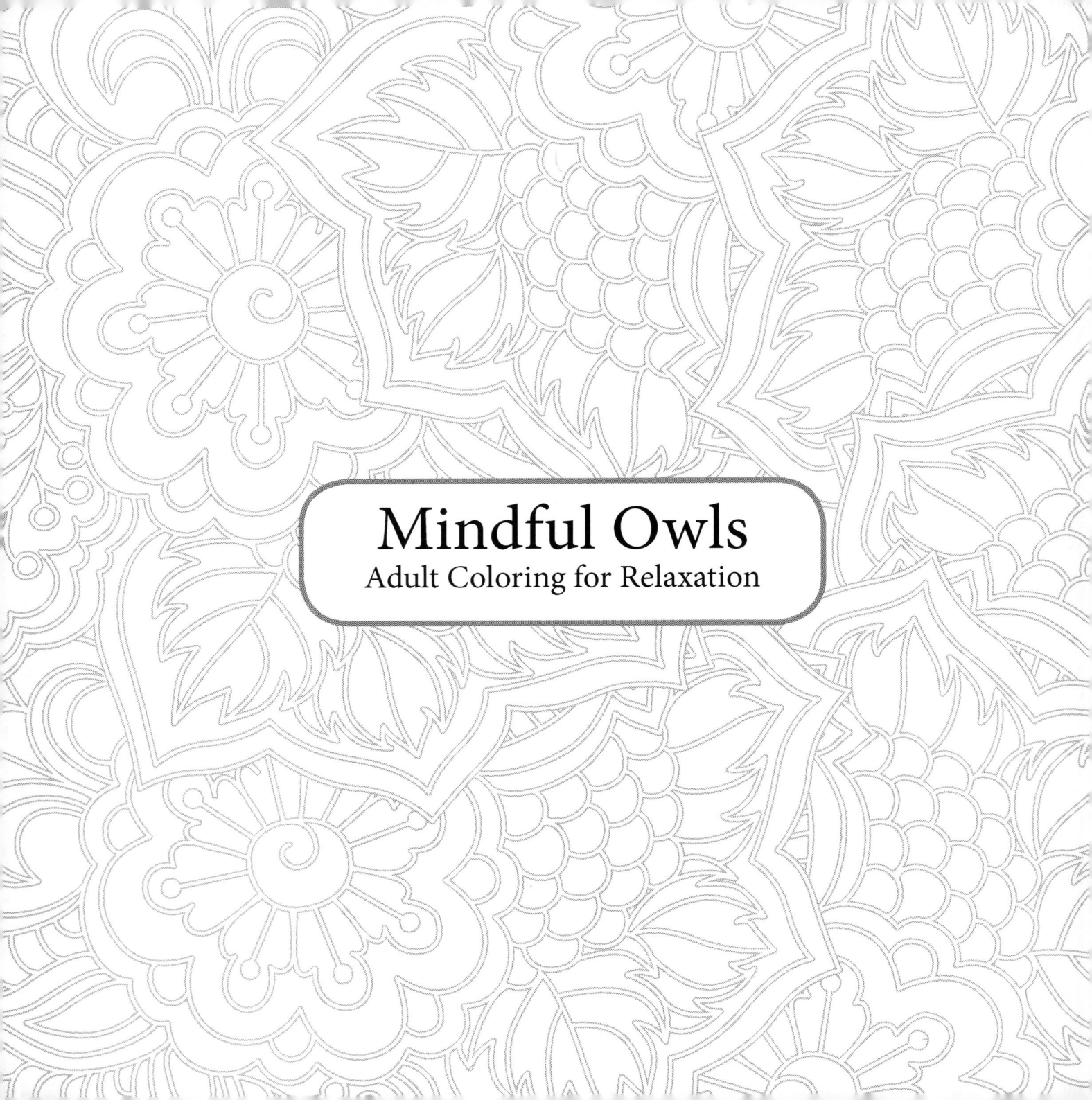

Mindful Owls
Adult Coloring for Relaxation

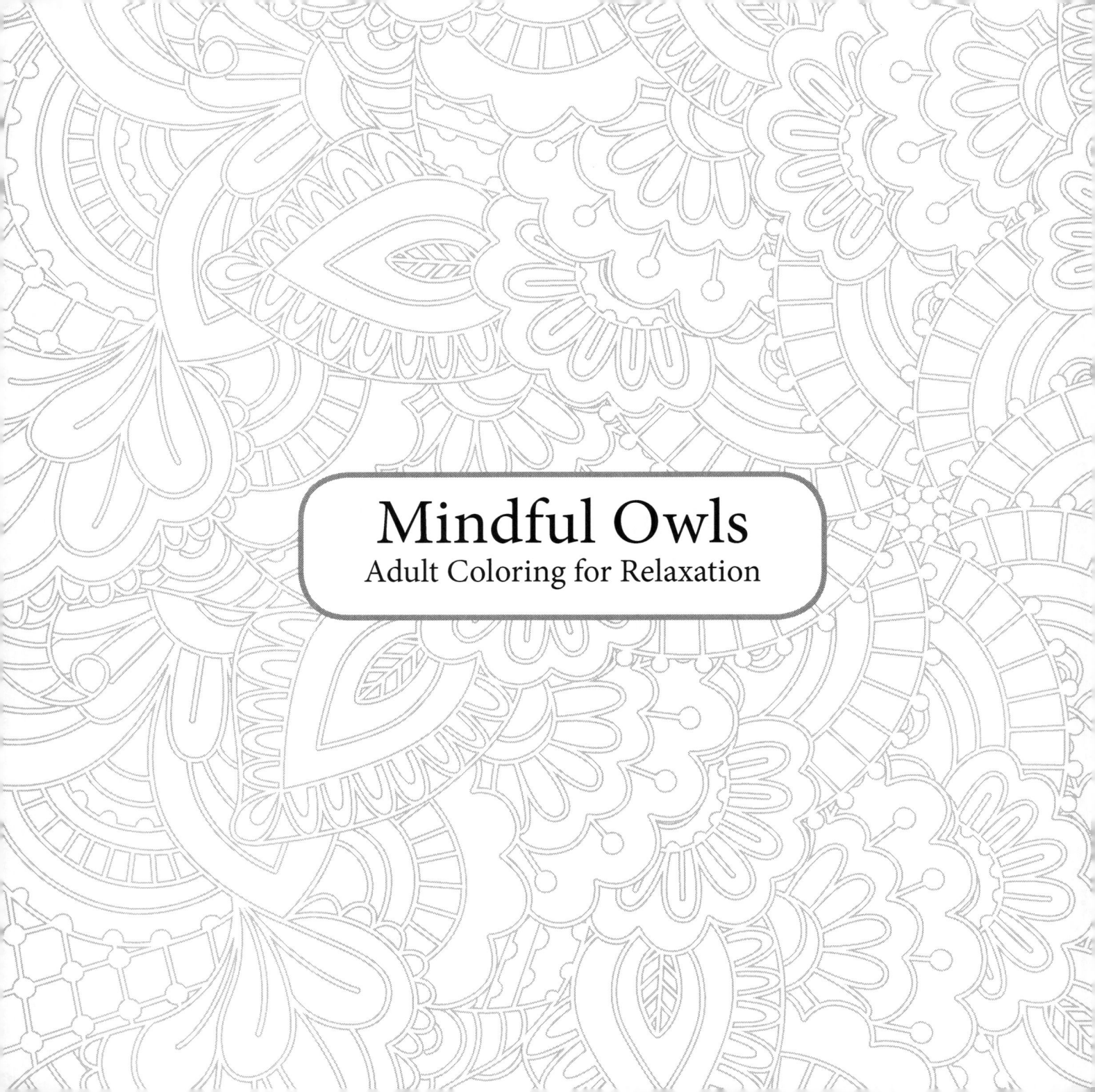

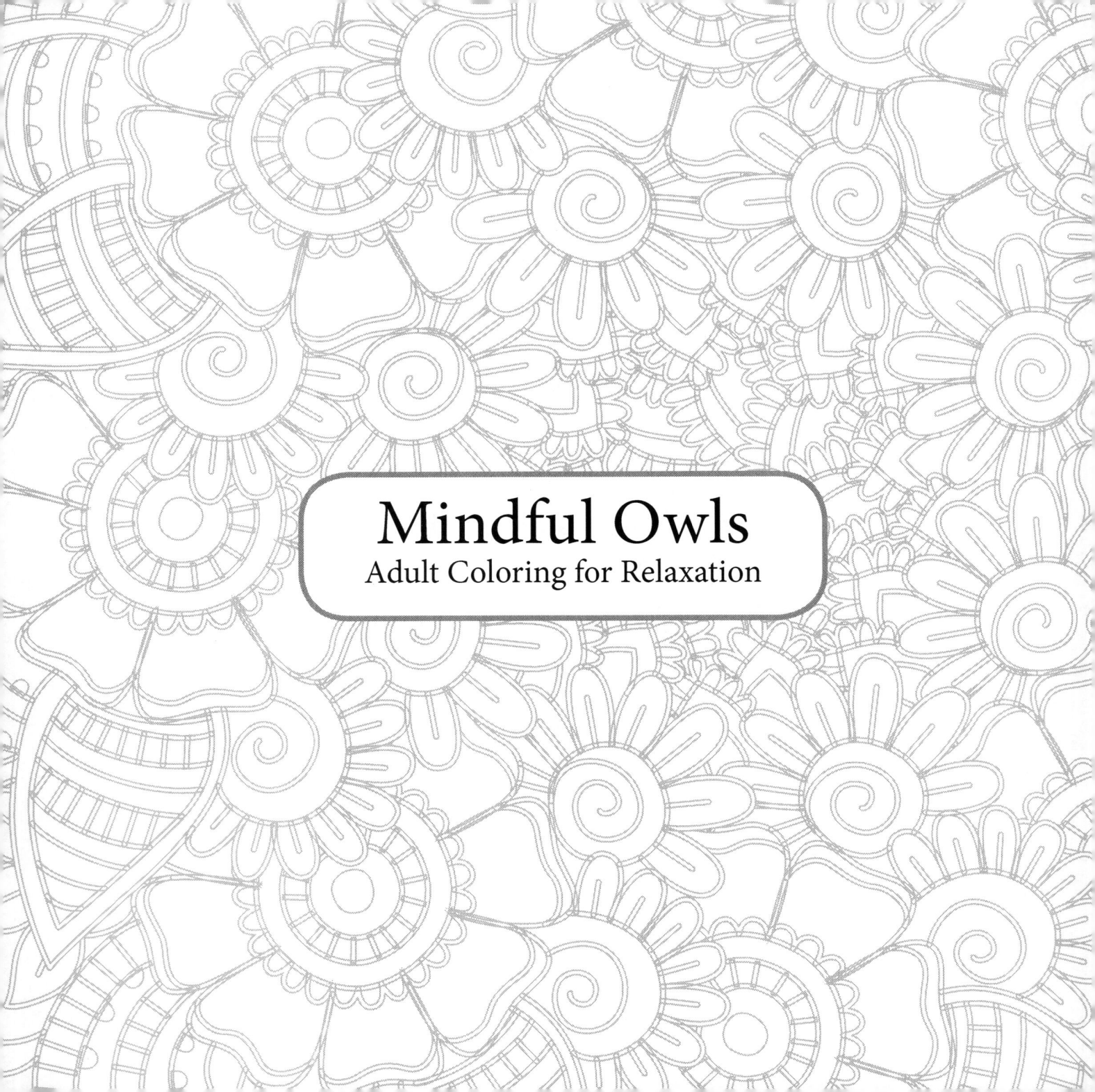

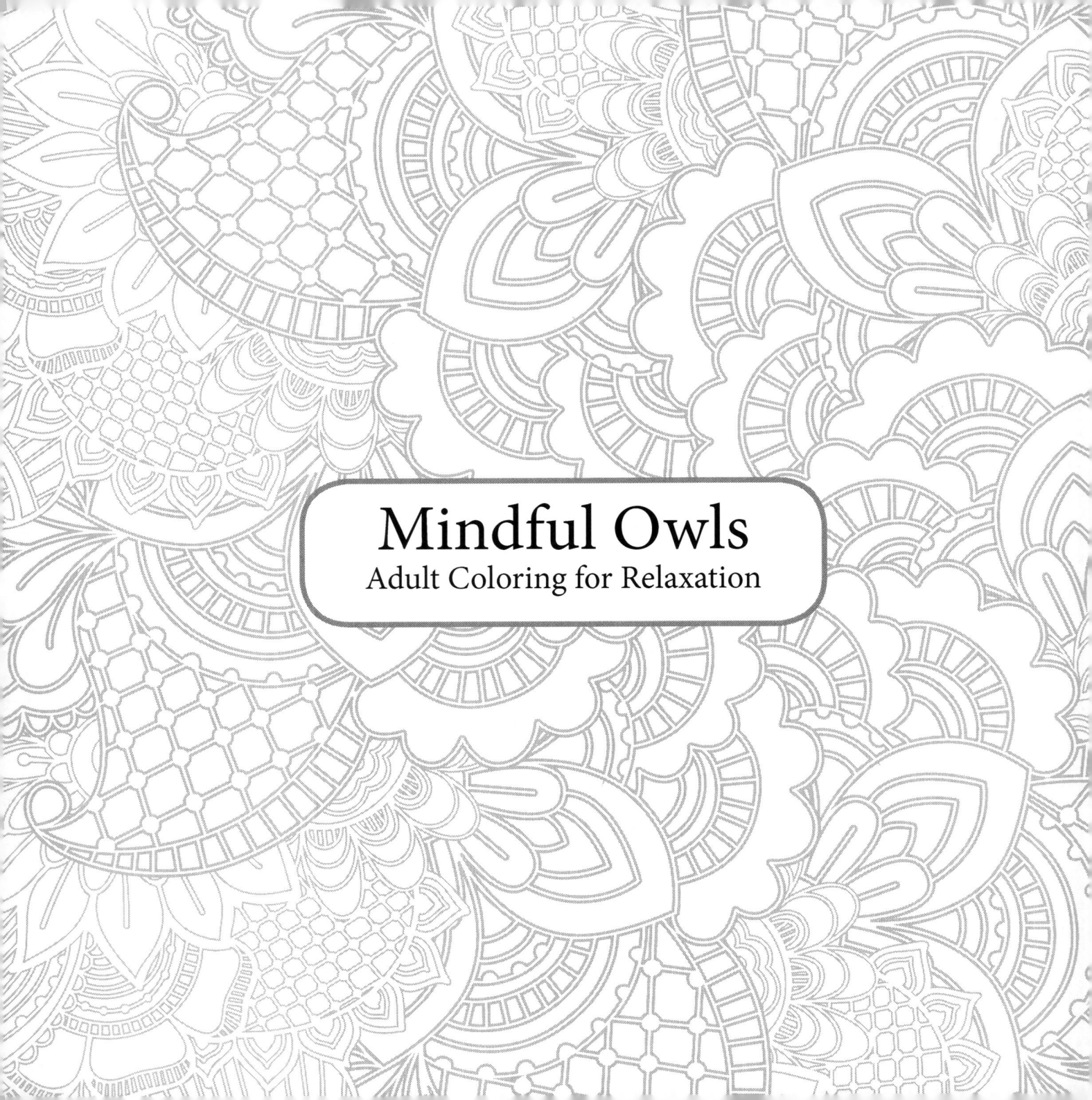

Interlude

You have a voice

Are you enjoying your experience? The world wants to hear your voice! Whether you love or loath this book, your feedback can make all the difference when someone is deciding whether it's right for them! When you have the opportunity, please visit Amazon or your favourite social network and share your thoughts by leaving a review or rating of this book.

Thank you,

Jack

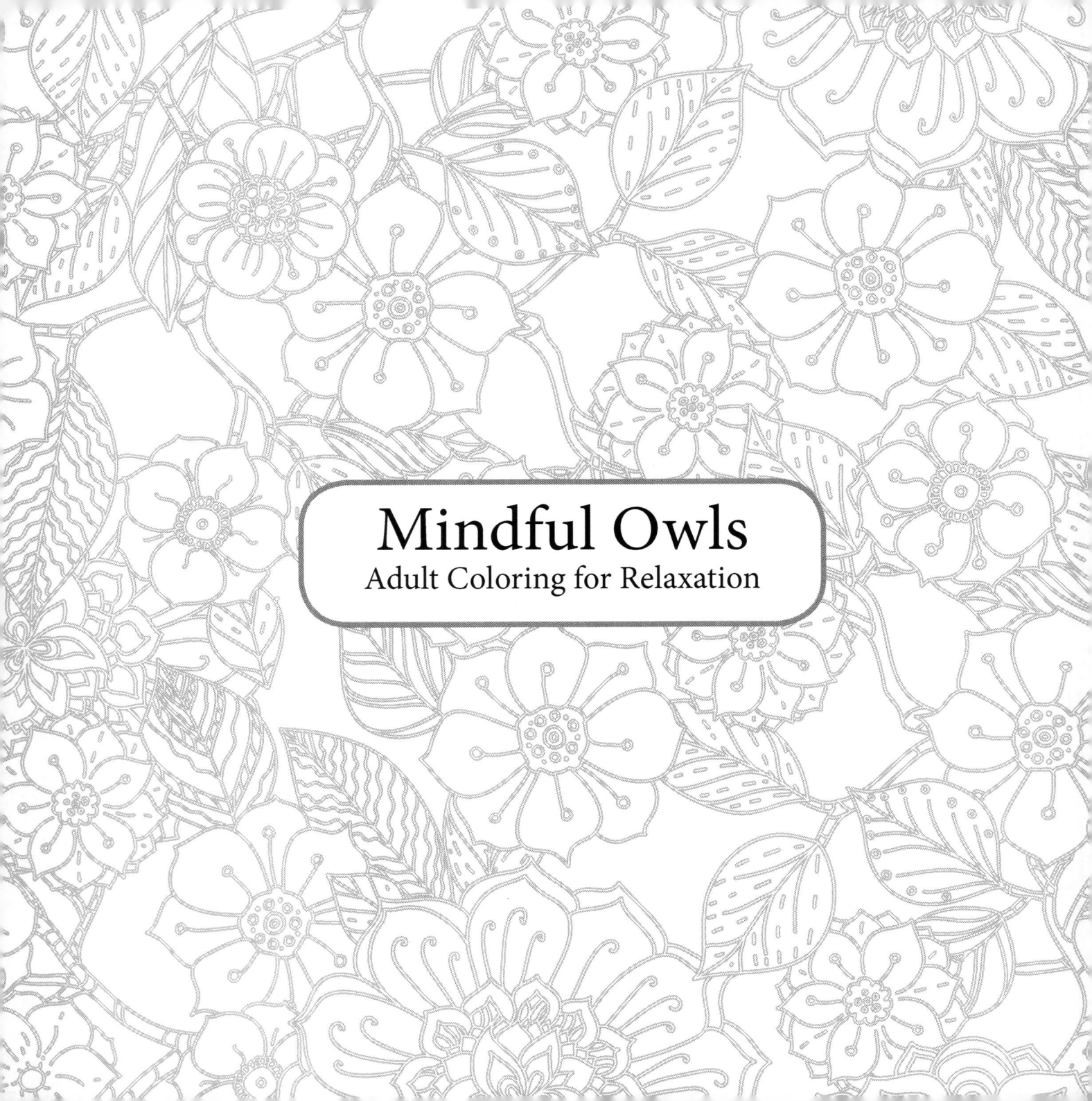

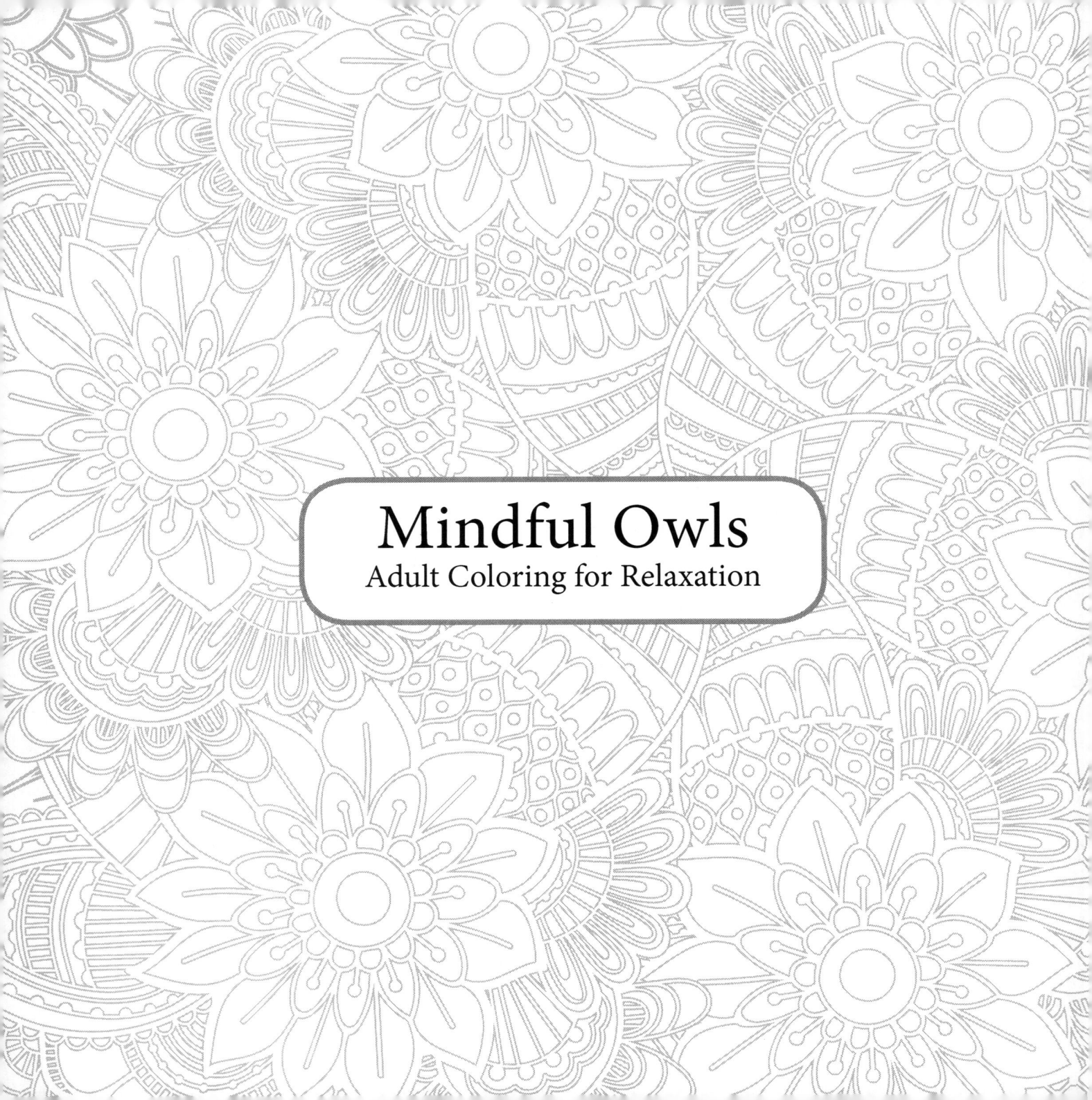
Mindful Owls
Adult Coloring for Relaxation

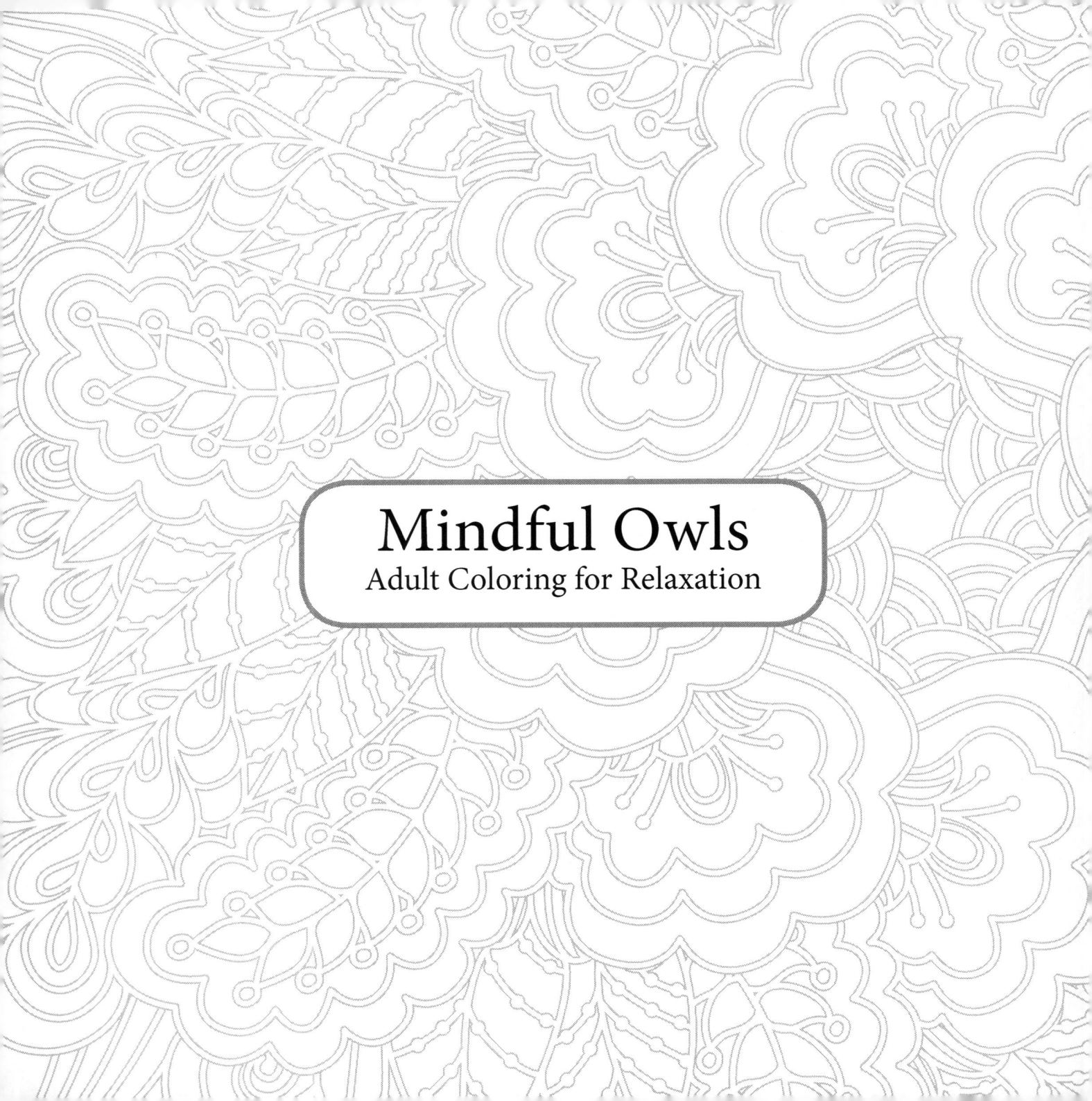

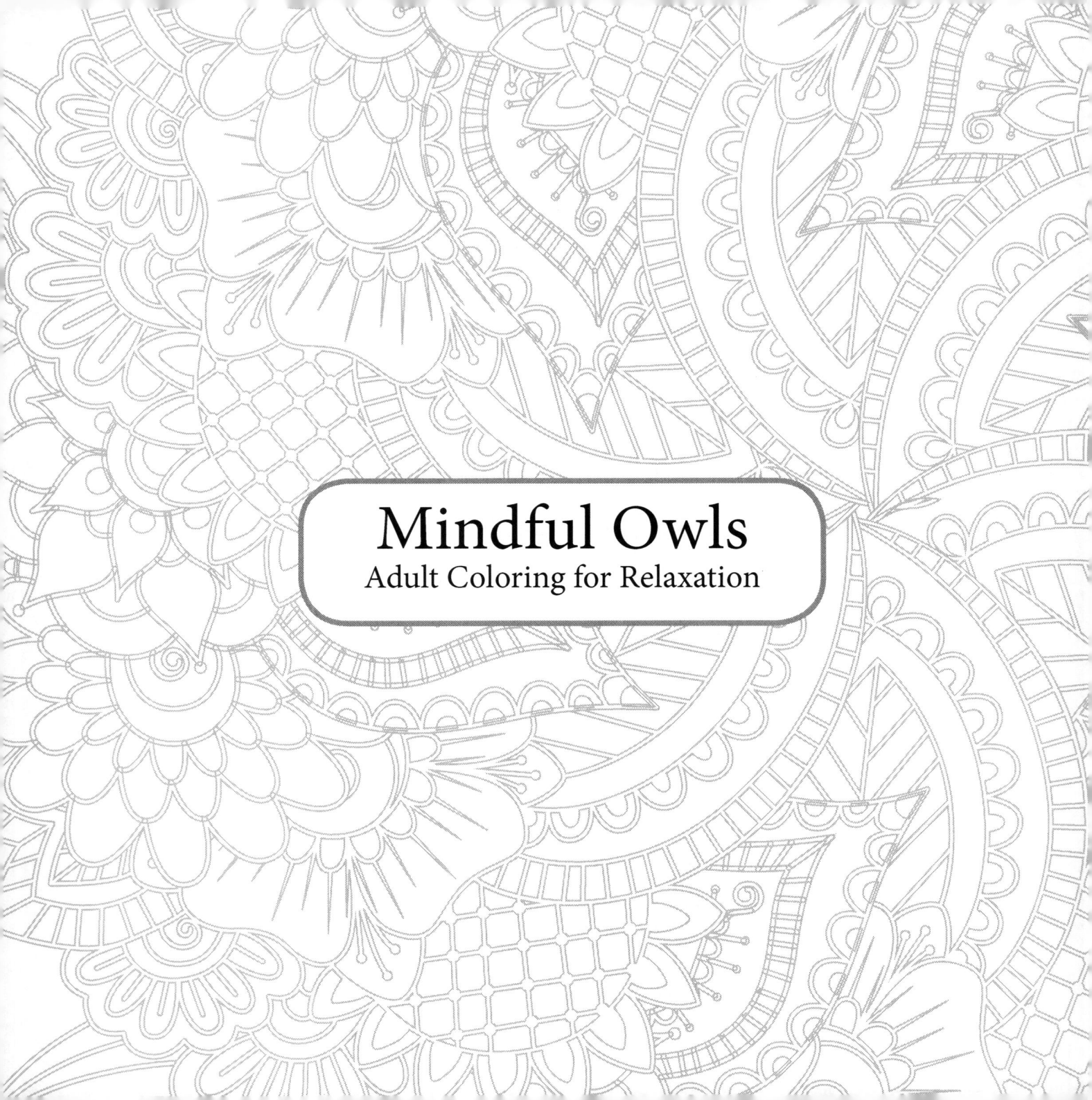

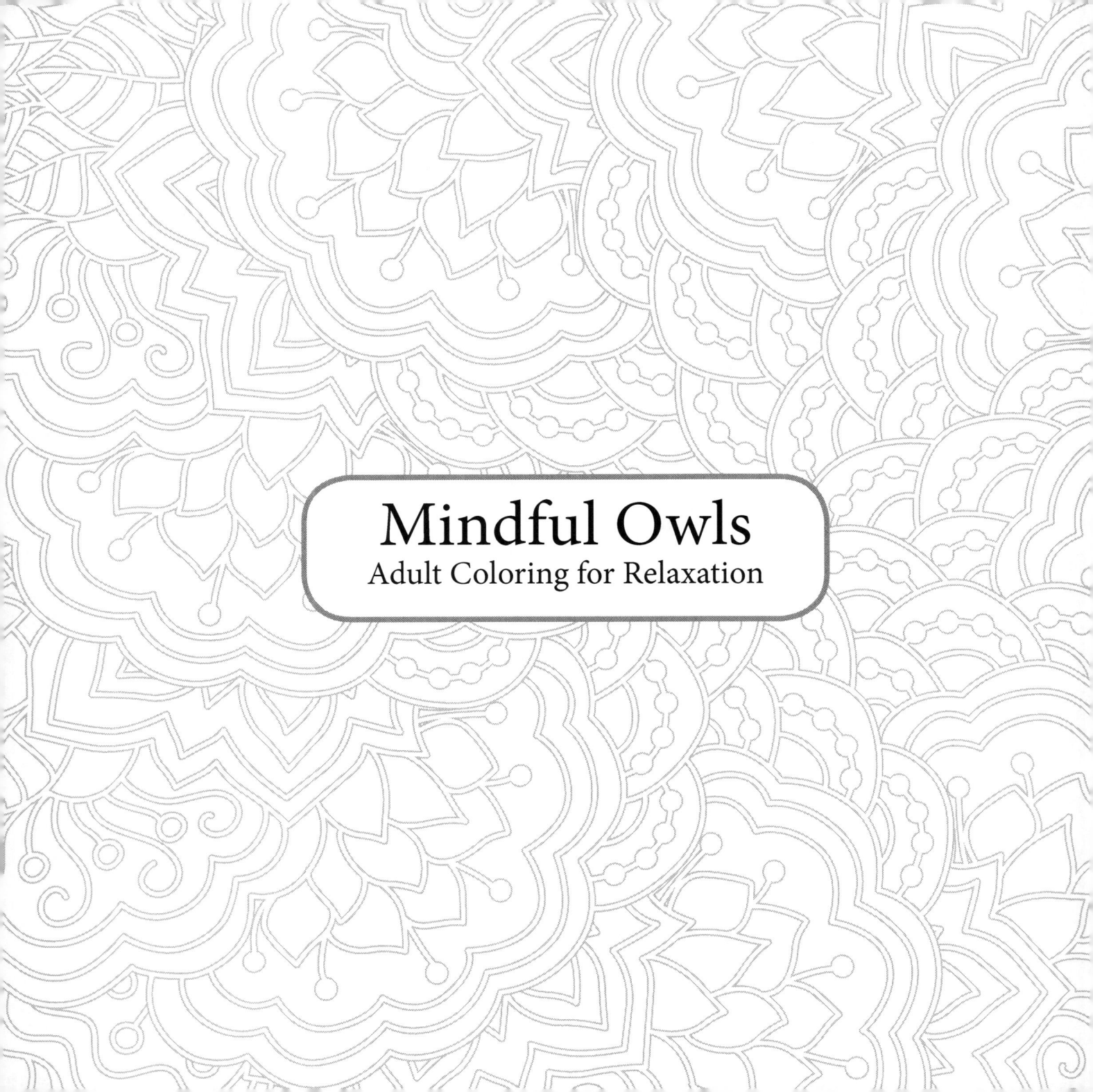

Mindful Owls
Adult Coloring for Relaxation

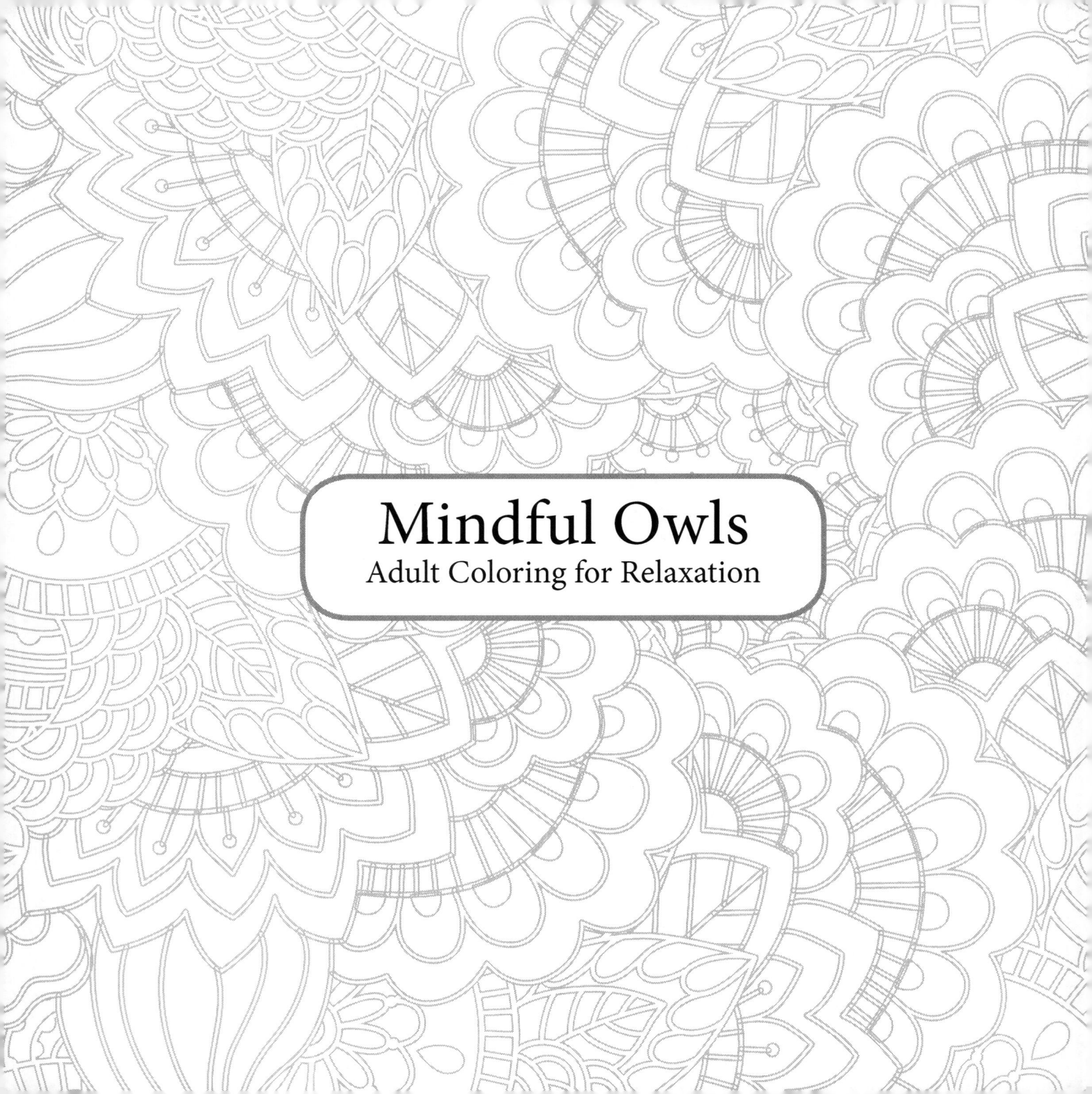

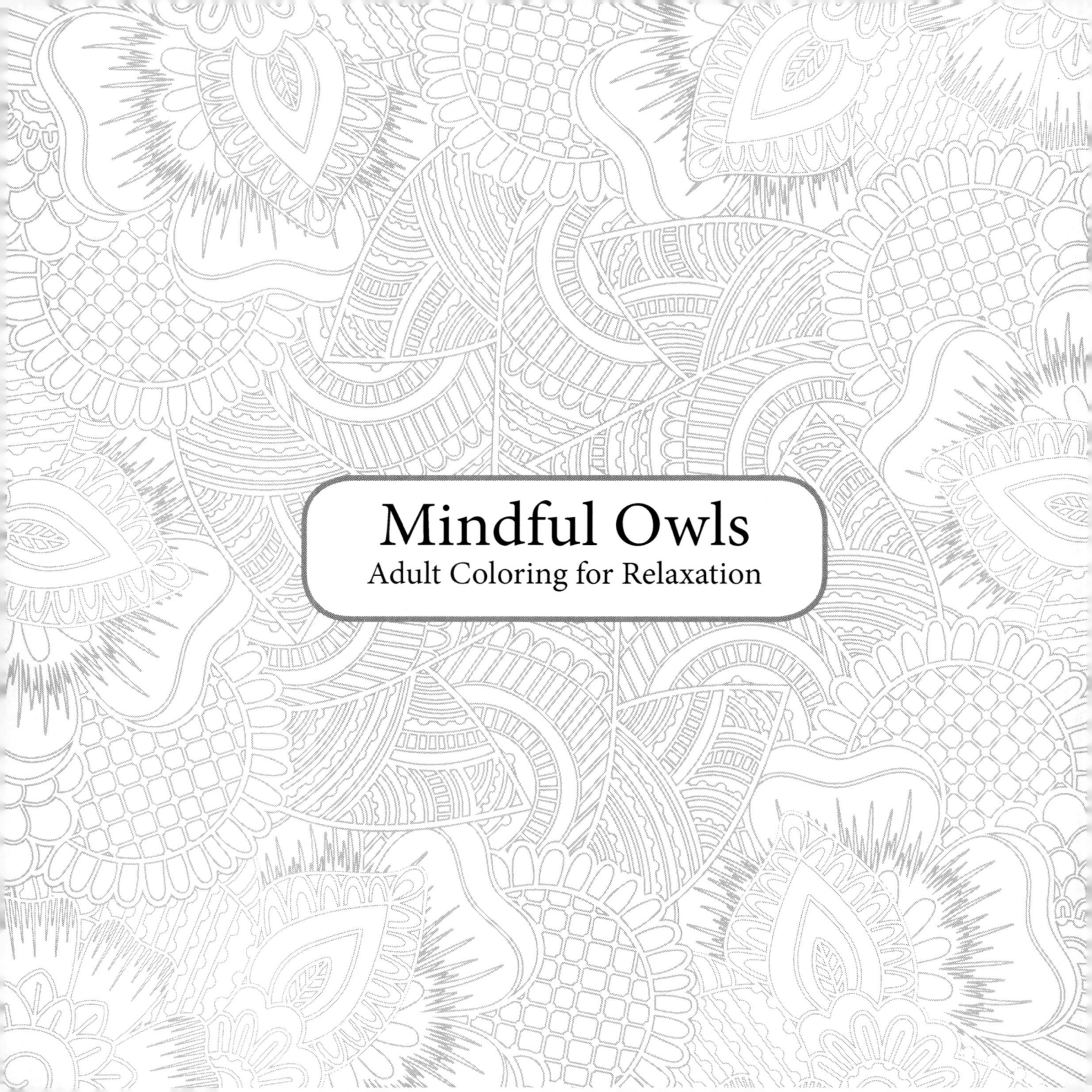

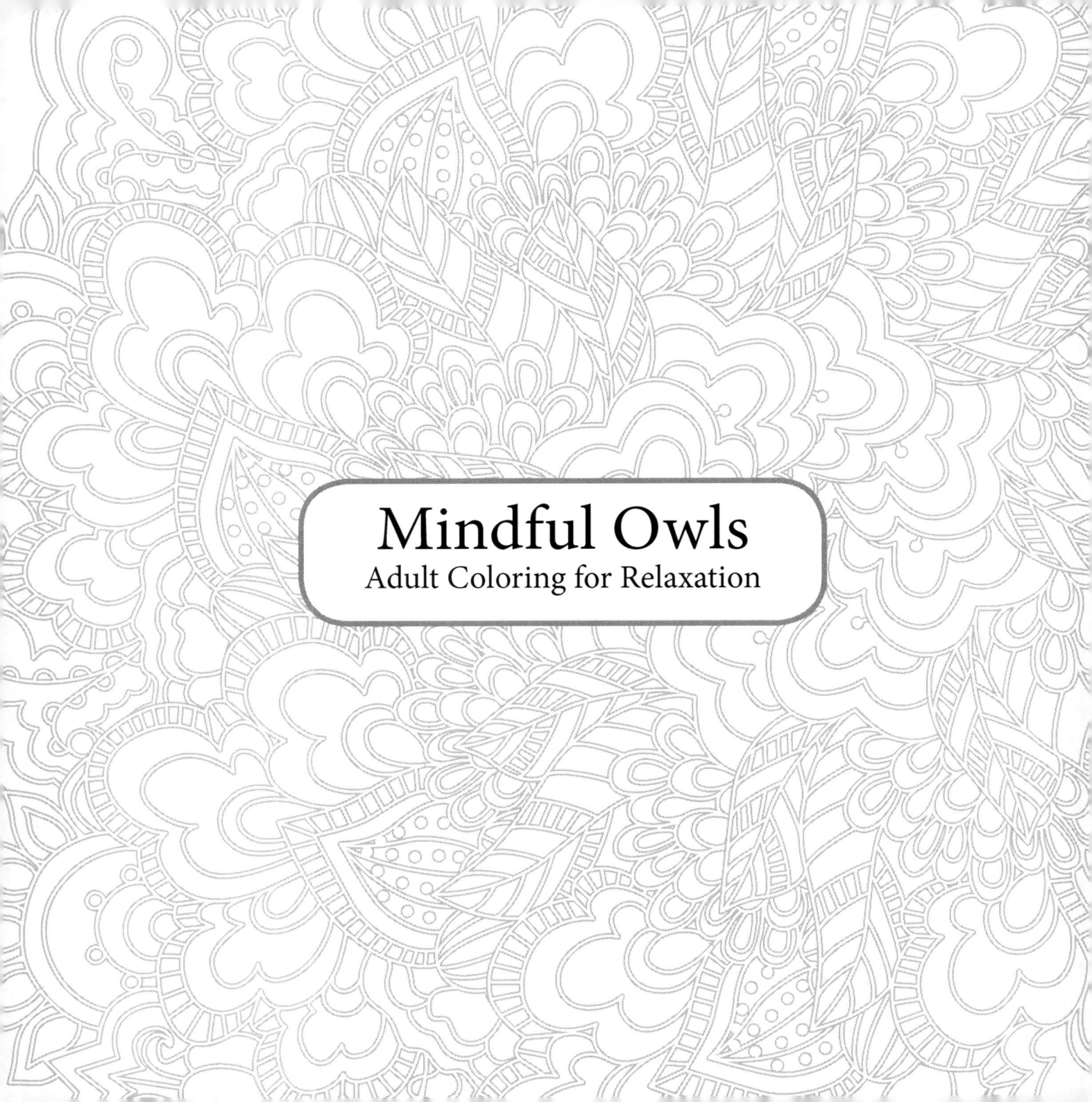

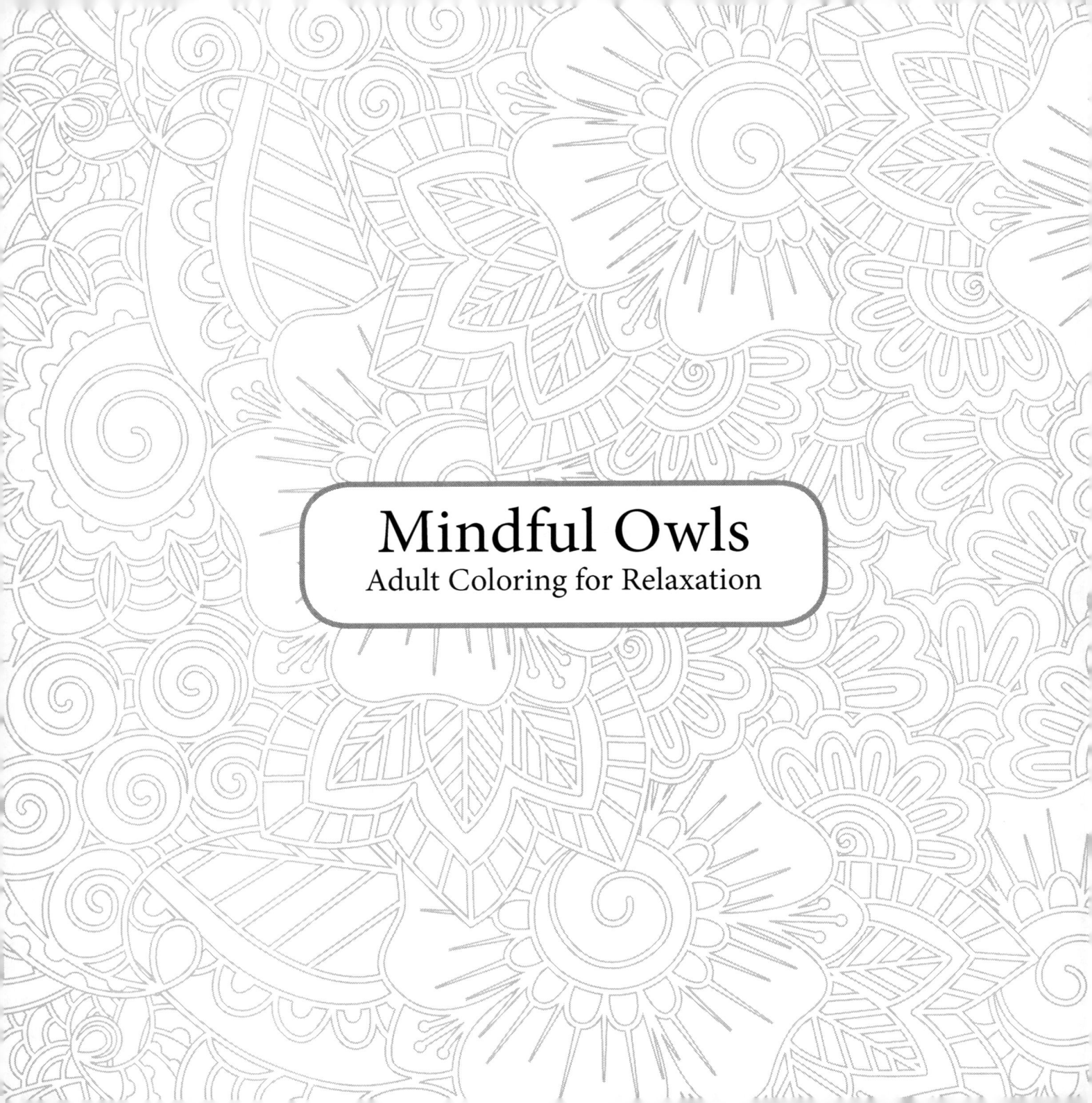

Now that you've completed this book, why not cut out your favourite patterns and share them with the people you care about...

Other books that may be of interest:

Colour Me Zen: Tranquility
Adult Colouring for Relaxation
by J. Benson

Colour Me Zen: Celtic Designs
Adult Colouring for Relaxation
by J. Benson

Colour Me Zen: Ancient Egypt
Adult Colouring for Relaxation
by J. Benson

Colour Me Zen: Mayan Mandalas
Adult Colouring for Relaxation
by J. Benson

available on Amazon now!

Illustrations
Copyright © 2015

Jack Benson
Dovile Kuusiene
Olesya Karakotsya
Alex Makarova
K Chung tw
Inna Artanova
Mariia Brzhezinskaia

Printed in Great Britain
by Amazon